25
Simple Things to Do
for
Literacy

Adapted from
*More Than 100 Tools for
Literacy in Today's Classroom.*

Joan F. Groeber

PEARSON
SkyLight

25 Simple Things to Do for Literacy

Published by Pearson Professional Development
1900 E. Lake Ave., Glenview, IL 60025
800-348-4474 or 847-657-7450
Fax 847-486-3183
info@pearsonpd.com
http://www.pearsonpd.com

ISBN 1-57517-828-1

3101UG
ZYXWVUTSRQPONMLKJIHGFEDCB
08 07 06 05 04 03   15 14 13 12 11 10 9 8 7 6 5 4 3

There are
one-story intellects,
  two-story intellects, and
    three-story intellects with skylights.

All fact collectors, who have no aim beyond their
facts, are
          one-story minds.

          Two-story minds
      compare, reason, generalize,
        using the labors of the fact collectors
              as well as their own.

              Three-story minds
idealize, imagine, predict—their best illumination
comes from above,

                    through the skylight.

—Oliver Wendell Holmes

Contents

Introduction

Classroom activities and exercises must be not only learner-centered but geared to the development and mastery of students' decision-making and problem-solving skills. The activities in *25 Simple Things to Do for Literacy* provide a starting point for teachers to develop their own activities based on the needs of their students. The metacognitive aspects of the exercises encourage students to reflect on what they did and what they learned and to discuss what they got out of the exercises. The activities share the following basic strategies rooted in metacognitive study.

* Instruction in any given topic must begin at the learner's level of experience.

* Long-term retention of any information occurs only when the information has meaning in the learner's life.

* Provide learners with tasks that go beyond simple recall.

* Use strategies that invite a broad range of responses.

* Understanding why and how we learn is an integral part of the learning process.

* Failure is viewed as a step in the process.

#1
What's in a Name?

BACKGROUND   Authors of fiction and poetry count on a catchy or thought-provoking title to appeal to their prospective audience. They create this title with great care to capture the essence of the material and provide clues about what they hope readers will come away with after reading the work.

ACTIVITY   Ask students to select a poem, short story, or novel to read alone or as a group. After they've read the work, have students compose a new title for it. Remind them that the title is the reader's first impression of the material, and if it is boring or misrepresents the work, the reader will be disappointed and less likely to return to that author for additional stories or poetry. Share the new titles as a class, discussing the reasons behind these choices. Use questions such as the following to help students reflect on their decision-making processes.

* What piece(s) of information found in the text led them to create the title?

* How important is the number and/or order of words in a title in capturing readers' interest? Why do they think that is true?

* What expectations did the original title create for them?

* What expectations do they think the new title will create for readers?

* How is the new title the same as or different from the original title?

* What role does a title play in your own choice of reading material?

#2
Heads Up

BACKGROUND   Authors of nonfiction also use the work's title to stimulate the interest of prospective readers. The title offers a quick, inviting glance into what the text contains. Students can mine this gold nugget of information to learn more about what is coming in the pages ahead.

ACTIVITY   Before they begin to read nonfiction text, ask students to convert chapter titles or the headings found within a chapter into questions. Depending on the length of the book and the grade level, focus on just the first chapter or cover the entire book. A book on earthquakes, for example, might have the following chapters: "Looking at the Earth," "Fault Lines," "The Causes of Earthquakes," "The Effects of Earthquakes," "Ring of Fire," and "Controlling Earthquakes." By converting these chapter titles into the following questions, readers identify their purpose for reading: to learn the answers to these questions.

* What does the earth look like?
* What are fault lines?
* What causes earthquakes?
* What are the effects of earthquakes?
* What is the ring of fire, and what does it have to do with earthquakes?
* How can we control earthquakes?

As they read a chapter as a group or independently, remind students to look for the answer(s) to their title question(s) in the material. After they finish reading, discuss as a group the possible answers to the title questions.

#3

Back to Front

BACKGROUND Review questions at the end of the chapter in some texts help students think about the important ideas in the passage. Located at the end of the chapter or section, however, they offer this insight after students have read the material. When students review the questions before reading the section, they can see what's important before they begin and can determine their purpose for reading the passage.

ACTIVITY With students working independently or in pairs, have them turn to the end of a section in their text and read the review questions found there. Have them select one question and read the text, seeking the response to this question. Have them note as they read which part of the text contained the information they needed to answer the question. Was it at the beginning? Many authors place the most vital information in the first few lines or paragraphs. Was it near the end? Authors often provide a summary statement to restate the most essential facts as an aid to the reader. Discuss the activity and students' findings as a class. Ask the class if reading the review questions first helped them understand the focus of the passage.

If students have trouble answering the review questions, break the questions down, focusing on key words and phrases in each question. Are students clear on the meaning of the terms? If not, work with students to identify the key term in each review question, then determine its meaning and its relationship to the concept presented in the text.

#4
Just Like Me

BACKGROUND Readers' understanding of a story increases if they are able to identify some link between themselves and the main character. In this way, they step into the story and view the events from a perspective of the reactions and emotions they share with the main character.

ACTIVITY Ask students to think about the main character as they read a story. Have them answer the following questions: In what ways is that character similar to you? In what ways are the two of you different?

Have students create a Venn diagram to illustrate the results. When students, working independently or in pairs, create the diagram, they must make decisions about which pieces of information will fit in each section of the graphic. The process of categorizing and writing responses reinforces the purpose of the activity.

CHARACTER
- Likes history class
- Can't get on sports team at new school
- Has no close relatives in area
- Wants parent to remarry
- Writes poetry

- No siblings
- Just moved to town
- Collect baseball cards
- Like to ride bicycle on long, empty stretches of road
- Get nervous meeting new people

READER
- Likes science class
- Plays sports on school team
- Lives next door to cousins
- Doesn't want divorced parent to remarry

#5
If I Were You ...

BACKGROUND   Students become more actively
involved in reading a story if they have
an opportunity to express their opinions about the characters' actions. They may, for example, have an approach to
resolving the story conflict that is very different from that
taken by the main character but very logical in their mind.
This exercise is extremely valuable in gaining insight to student thought processes and motivation.

ACTIVITY   Ask students to envision themselves as the
main character while they read. Then in
a class discussion or written exercise, have them assume
the identity of the story's main character and respond to
questions such as the following, which help them focus on
problem-solving skills.

* What, in your opinion, is the biggest obstacle or
  challenge you face? Why?
* How do you plan to tackle it? What is the first
  step you'll take?
* What special talents or abilities are necessary to
  solve this problem? Which, if any, of these skills
  do you possess?
* Whom can you rely on for help?
* How will your life change if you attain your
  goal? What will happen if you don't?

#6

Picture This

BACKGROUND The best picture books use the text and illustrations as storytelling partners. Young children hearing bedtime stories from their parents are so eager for a visualization of the characters and events that, when the parent relates a tale from memory, the child interrupts constantly for more detailed descriptions of what the princess looked like or how tall the castle stood. For beginning readers, illustrations offer key insights into understanding what the written text contains. In the case of more mature readers, the pictures enhance the sensory experience.

ACTIVITY Have students select their favorite picture book. Ask them to look carefully at the illustrations in the story. Then on paper or in a class discussion, have them list at least eight details the pictures provide that aren't found in the text.

ENRICHMENT Cover the words in any picture book, and have students try to tell as much of the story as they can using only the illustrations. Have students respond to questions such as the following: How does the illustrator let you know how the main character feels about what is happening? Briefly describe the setting and tell how important it is to the events of the story. For example, dark, rainy nights are usually more crucial to the plot than bright, sunny afternoons. List three details not directly related to appearance that you learned about the main character simply by looking at the pictures. What clues led you to your opinion?

#7

That's Your Cue

BACKGROUND   Readers can learn a lot about characters from the words used to describe how they speak, such as *he shouted* or *she explained slowly*. These phrases give us hints about that person's personality: happy, impatient, rude, and so on. Since books are not ordinarily an auditory medium (except in the case of audio books), these emotive phrases suggest to the reader the tone, speed, and inflection the speaker used. Readers compare this information with what they know about real-life speech patterns and make decisions about what emotions the characters are experiencing throughout the story.

ACTIVITY   Have students select a character other than the main character and jot down five phrases that describe how he or she speaks. Ask them to use those words to form three conclusions about that person's personality. For example, one might describe a character whose conversation includes such adverbs as *calmly, slowly,* or *gently* as a patient person.

Ask students to reflect on their conclusions and try to think of someone they know who is like that character. How would they feel about having that character as a friend? Why? Have students share their ideas with classmates in a group discussion of the book.

#8

Taste Tempters

(Description)

BACKGROUND Most learners rely only on the senses of sight and sound to identify and categorize new information. Yet the three remaining senses—taste, touch, smell—hold a wealth of additional information to expand and enhance the learner's perception of an object or concept.

Texts written in the description mode use all five senses to bring the topic to life for readers. These texts often supply the backbone of a reader's knowledge on a given topic, for through description, most concepts are introduced to young readers. Recognizing a book organized in this format prepares learners to receive information with all five senses.

ACTIVITY One of the most effective means of understanding the structure of a text is to replicate it. Descriptive texts contain information gathered from using all five senses; therefore, writing a descriptive passage requires sharpening of all the senses.

Have students write a description of their favorite food. The description must use all five senses but must not name the food. Then have them read the descriptions aloud to see if their classmates can guess the favorite food.

#9

Dressed for Success
(Sequence)

BACKGROUND   Recipes contain a prescribed sequence, or order, of instructions; so do building projects from constructing a birdhouse to building a skyscraper. Even jokes and stories are told in sequence, using such words as *first, next,* and *finally.*

Like a sequenced activity, the order of a sequence text is essential to understanding the material and producing the desired outcome. Reversal or omission of steps means failure for both reader and writer and, depending on the subject matter, can result in minor errors or prove disastrous. The success or failure of a sequence text is the easiest of the five basic structures to gauge objectively. If a reader follows the sequence exactly but does not achieve the desired outcome, the fault lies with the writer.

ACTIVITY   Every day, people perform tasks that require them to use a specific sequence. Have students list, in writing, how they dress for school in the morning, numbering each step. Then have them switch two of the steps and predict the outcome. Then ask them to omit a step and think about how they'd look when they arrived at school. Share their findings as a class.

#10

Here and There

(Comparison)

BACKGROUND Texts organized in a comparison structure encourage readers to look at each idea or topic in its component parts, sifting through the data for similarities and differences among the concepts presented.

This activity gives students practice in the process of accommodation, comparing two or more objects or ideas by focusing on their differences. Accommodation requires a more mature level of thought process than comparison that focuses on similarities (assimilation) because students must first establish criteria for comparison then identify the discrepancies. For example, when comparing two schoolrooms, students may find the two rooms have the same number of windows (similarity), but the windows in one room are smaller (difference).

ACTIVITY Have students list five ways the classroom is different from their bedroom. Then ask them to list ways the rooms are alike. Remind them to think in terms of the rooms' function, size, furnishings, regular occupants, visitors, and decorations. When they have finished, discuss as a class the following questions: Which list was easier to make? Why do they think this is so?

Repeat the activity, using two rooms in the same building such as separate classrooms at school, two rooms in the students' home, and so on. Then discuss these questions: Was composing these lists easier or more difficult compared with the first lists they made? What do they think is the reason for the difference? Have students compare and discuss the lists in small groups.

#11

Why Do You Think This Is So?

(Cause and Effect)

BACKGROUND "For every action, there is an equal and opposite reaction," Newton's third law of motion says, and the truth of the statement is evident in our daily lives. Pulling down on the cord of window blinds makes the blinds go up. Hitting an oncoming tennis ball with a tennis racquet causes the ball to travel in the opposite direction.

Texts organized in cause-and-effect structure either identify the effect, then examine the causes that led to it, or explore the elements required to bring about a certain outcome or event. In both cases, a good writer clearly defines the connection between the cause and the effect.

ACTIVITY Have students reflect on cause and effect in their own lives. Ask them to think of something that has happened to them recently, then list, in writing, three to four reasons (causes) the event occurred.

Next, ask them to examine their behavior in class, with friends, or on the playing field, and, in writing, explain what effect they think their actions have on them socially or on their performance on and off the field. What outcome do they hope for in these different situations? How can they alter their actions to produce the desired outcome (effect)?

#12

What's the Problem?

(Problem and Solution)

BACKGROUND Everyone has problems. Some we can solve on our own, others require help from someone else. Still other problems may be beyond our control entirely.

Texts organized in problem-and-solution format identify the problem early in the text. The author explains whether the problem is easy or difficult to solve and offers some suggestions for managing the dilemma. Finally, readers learn how to implement the steps necessary to solve the problem.

ACTIVITY Make time for this activity both now and in a few weeks so students can check their problem-solving progress.

Students will agree that almost everybody has at least one thing they'd like to change about themselves, and though it's important to like ourselves, there's nothing wrong with wanting to try to do something better. Have students think about a habit or characteristic they have that they really don't like, such as interrupting someone who is speaking, always being late for dinner, and so on. In their journals, have them state the problem they have identified and offer at least three solutions to reduce or eliminate the problem. Be sure they date their entries.

Check back on the entry in a few weeks or months. Ask students to prepare a new journal entry reporting their success in making the change. If changing the behavior has been a struggle, have them try to think of some other strategies that might help. If they changed the behavior successfully, ask them to describe the process—was it difficult? Did they have to modify any of their original solutions, or did they accomplish the behavior change by using those solutions?

#13

Weather or Not

(Charts and Graphs)

BACKGROUND   Charts and graphs provide readers with an at-a-glance way to grasp and retain sizable amounts of information, particularly numerical data. Organized so readers can compare data easily, these graphic features highlight the relationship among the data clearly and concisely.

To teach students how information is organized in a graph or chart, have them gather data through an informal survey and display the data by using one of these features. Seeing firsthand how information is accumulated for use on a graph or chart helps readers know what to look for when they encounter one in an expository passage.

ACTIVITY   Have students record the daily high and low temperatures in your city or town for a week by using a line graph and two colored markers: red for high temperatures, blue for low. At the end of the week, have one student connect the high temperatures with the red marker and another student connect the low temperatures with the blue marker.

Have students examine the graph to answer the following questions. Do the lines ever intersect? On what days? On what day does the greatest temperature difference occur? On what day does the smallest temperature difference occur? How many, if any, different days have identical highs and lows?

Then have students write a two- to three-sentence description of this week's weather using information they obtained from the graph.

#14

Take a Second Look

(Illustrations)

BACKGROUND Many readers, even seasoned veterans of the printed word, often skip over photos in expository text in their desire to hurry to the end of a passage or chapter. In doing so, they pass up the opportunity to view myriad pieces of relevant information a single photo contains. Ironically, nonreaders build a great deal of a passage's meaning based on illustrations, while mature learners often dismiss them as filler, taking space away from the more highly valued printed word. Photos and sketches possess the power to breathe life into a page filled with print, but only if readers pay them the attention they deserve.

ACTIVITY Instruct students to select a picture from a nonfiction text and list seven things they notice when they look at the picture. Encourage them to look beyond just the objects in the picture; for example, instead of writing "a lady in a blue dress," "a brown and white cow," and so on, they might say, "the lady is smiling," or "the cow looks too thin." Such a list requires more student judgment (Why do you think the cow looks too thin?) and might, therefore, produce a more thorough examination of the picture paired with the reader's prior knowledge. Have them describe what they think the passage is about based on the picture.

Read the passage associated with the picture aloud in class, and ask students to reexamine their lists to add something they learned about the picture from reading the text. Discuss whether the picture helped them better understand the text. Were their predictions about the content based on the picture accurate?

#15

Help Wanted

BACKGROUND   As mature readers get to know the characters in a story, they begin comparing them, unconsciously, with individuals in their own lives. Readers might also compare a character with one they encountered in another book. As they organize information about the characters, they are better able to imagine them in situations beyond the printed story. When readers can manipulate characters outside the parameters of the story world, they develop a better understanding of how the characters' virtues and shortcomings affect their choices in their fictional lives.

ACTIVITY   Tell students to write a classified ad for the type of job the story's main character could do successfully. Remind them to think about the skills and abilities the character has displayed during the story. It might help them to think about how those attributes remind them of a real person and at what sort of job that individual excels.

VARIATION   Have students complete this activity with the main characters from a variety of books. Then have students post their ads on a class bulletin board along with the names of all the characters applying for employment, and let classmates guess which characters could respond to each ad. Discuss the traits each character possesses so students can make educated guesses about which character could fill each position.

#16
Remember When . . .

BACKGROUND   Students' background knowledge leads
them to retain and discard certain
information they receive while reading a story. Unfortun-
ately, what they may consider the most important details
may not be those the teacher highlights for use in future
evaluations. It is important, however, to recognize what kind
of and how much information students retain from a story
to assess their level of comprehension. Immature readers
tend to focus on a single, minute detail, assigning it much
greater importance than a pivotal scene or character.
Having some idea of what each reader considers important
provides a clearer picture of his or her ability to read with
real understanding.

ACTIVITY   Have students list ten characteristics of a
story's main character. Answers might
range from the way he or she laughs to the number of siblings he or she has to how the character feels about a certain
issue such as school, animals, and so on.

After they have completed their lists, place students into
groups of three to five students. Ask them to compare lists
and answer the following questions: Did each of you remem-
ber the same characteristics? Do any of the group's members
have identical or very similar lists? Do you have something
completely different on your list? If so, why did that fact
stand out in your mind?

Discuss the lists with the whole class to see if anyone
remembered something that no one else did.

#17

To Whom It May Concern

BACKGROUND   By the time most students have finished reading or listening to a story, they have some definite opinions about some other way the character's problem might have been resolved. Students are only too willing to take charge of a story, planning and executing a different, and in their opinion, more satisfying, ending. Mining those ideas provides teachers with an excellent opportunity to examine readers' decision-making skills and conflict-resolution thought processes.

ACTIVITY   Have students write a letter to the main character, offering some advice regarding his or her situation. It may be the character has not examined every avenue of action open to him or her. Remind students to think about the resources the character has at his or her disposal for solving the problem; for example, if the character is stranded in the wilderness, don't suggest taking the next bus to his or her neighborhood. Share the letters as a class, discussing some of the best options the main character might have taken to solve his or her problem more quickly.

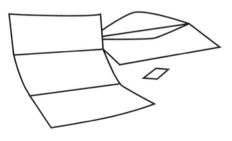

#18
It's an Honor

BACKGROUND   As readers learn more about the story's main character, they recognize his or her strengths and limitations and make judgments about whether they would want to know that person in real life. Most readers tend to focus on the character's strengths, such as athletic ability, intelligence, or bravery, as they begin to unconsciously project their own dreams and aspirations on that individual: "If I were like (character X), I'd be able to handle the bullies at school."

Finding activities that celebrate a character's positive attributes is a good first step in not only helping readers understand that character but providing a chance for them to focus on what traits they might want to develop as they mature.

ACTIVITY   Have students imagine that the story's main character is being honored at an awards banquet, and have them respond to the following questions in writing or in a class discussion. Why is the character being honored? Can you imagine how his or her acceptance speech might begin? Who will be there to cheer the character on?

Have students design a medal or award certificate for the character and explain what it represents. Display the medals or certificates on a class bulletin board.

#19
From the Beginning ...

BACKGROUND Readers are asked to predict what will happen next in a story. Many of the same thought processes are required to consider what might have brought the main character to the point where he or she was at the beginning of the story.

Thinking backwards is a great cause-and-effect activity: the effect is where the reader and character begin the story, while the time before the text begins might offer the reasons, or causes, the character finds himself or herself in this particular situation.

ACTIVITY Have students draw a picture of or write a paragraph about the main character in the hours or minutes before the actual story begins. Be sure they show or describe the emotion, such as happiness or fear, the character is experiencing as well as the activity he or she is engaged in at the start of the story. Have students tell what clues in the text tell them what to draw or write.

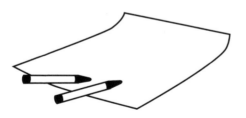

#20
Listen Up

BACKGROUND   Making good listening into a game encourages even the most reluctant student to get actively involved. Games generate a type of excitement not usually found in more conventional lessons. Such activities are especially beneficial after a long, silent written exercise, for students can talk without causing unwanted disruptions in the class.

ACTIVITY   Begin this listening chain with the phrase, "I went to the mall and bought . . . ," completing the sentence with the item purchased. Call on students randomly, and more than one time, challenging them to add their "purchases" to the existing shopping list, repeating aloud each item mentioned to that point in the game and in the correct order. Continue around the room until the chain is broken when someone is unable to repeat the sequence of items in the proper order. Allow the entire class to keep track, letting anyone who makes a mistake know about it right away, or appoint a designated listener to keep track of the items purchased.

VARIATION   Tailor this activity to particular units of study by altering the opening phrase: I drove across America and visited *name of city;* I went to the museum and saw *type of exhibit,* and so on.

#21
Alphabet Soup

BACKGROUND One of the most effective ways to organize auditory material is to listen for a definite pattern in the words or phrases. A group of words strung together is easier to recall if some organizer such as alphabetical order is included. This strategy works in many listening games, such as this activity where students play a round-robin–style game by using an alphabetical or numerical sequence.

ACTIVITY Select a category—in this example, it's grocery shopping—then introduce the listening chain with a statement containing a word that fits in the category and begins with the letter A: I went to the grocery store and bought an apple. Call on students randomly, and more than one time, if possible, challenging them to continue the chain by adding a word that fits in the category and begins with the letter B, then C, and so on. Each student must first repeat the earlier words in the sequence: apple, broccoli, carrots, doughnuts, eggs, fish, and so on. Continue the game until you reach the letter Z or the chain is broken when a student is unable to repeat the proper sequence of items.

CATEGORY IDEAS

* animals
* colors
* foods
* feelings
* clothing
* compound words
* vehicles
* first names
* famous places
* story characters
* school supplies
* careers

#22

Tongue Twisters

BACKGROUND   Word puzzles are a great way to get students excited about developing their vocabularies because these exercises are easy to understand and rooted in humor. Even the most reluctant learner cannot resist the challenge of figuring out the puzzle before anyone else. Puzzles and riddles provide a painless way to reinforce the concepts presented in class.

ACTIVITY   Homophones are words that sound alike but have different meanings. Have students try to guess the homophone pairs in each phrase either working alone or as a class.

EXAMPLE RIDDLES	ANSWERS
Rabbit fur	hare hair
Motionless writing paper	stationary stationery
Undecorated aircraft	plain plane
The entire cavity	whole hole
Tired vegetable	beat beet
Dessert for a caribou	moose mousse
60 minutes we spend together	our hour
Letters for boys and men	mail male
Naked cub	bare bear
The story of a dog's wagger	tale tail
A wobbly seven days	weak week
Authentic fishing gear	real reel
A stallion with a sore throat	hoarse horse
Drink for golfing equipment	tea tee
Disinterested wood plank	bored board
Female relative of a bug	ant aunt

#23

Ginonym

BACKGROUND A card game already familiar to students is an excellent foundation for constructing new vocabulary development activities. The games can focus on any one aspect of language such as compound words, affixes, and so on and be built around the rules of Hearts, Rummy, Go Fish, or Old Maid. For an added challenge, have students create the decks themselves. After writing the words on one side, they can draw the same picture on the back of every card in that deck. Have students work in groups of three or four to create the decks.

ACTIVITY Two to four students can play this variation of Gin Rummy, which involves synonyms and antonyms. Have students create a deck in multiples of three, using a pattern that offers a synonym and antonym for the same word. Some examples are Over–Above–Below, Huge–Big–Small, Complete–Entire–Partial, and Slim–Narrow–Wide.

The dealer deals each player five cards, then places the remaining cards in the middle of the table. Players draw and discard as they attempt to make synonym pairs (1 point) and antonym pairs (2 points) with their cards. Players wishing to take a card from the discard pile that is not on top of the stack must also collect any cards discarded after the desired card. Since synonym pairs are worth fewer points than antonym pairs, players may want to wait until they can make antonym pairs, but since only the winner's points are tallied, they must decide which choice to make. Play continues until one player reaches 25 points. As in rummy, players can lay down an antonym to go with another player's synonym cards or vice versa.

#24
Compound Rummy

BACKGROUND Student-created decks of word-play cards accomplish a number of classroom objectives. They provide highly stimulating drill practice for language concepts, and, because students actually create the cards, they involve students in more than one phase of the learning process. Creating room supplies such as the cards gives them a feeling of ownership, which makes the items and their use that much more appealing and motivating to students.

ACTIVITY Have students create a deck of compound words, separating each word onto two cards. For example, using the compound word *railroad, rail* would appear on one card and *road* on the second card. Place students in groups of no more than six players. Make sure each deck contains no fewer than thirty pairs of compound words.

With students in groups of three to five players, have them appoint a dealer who distributes five cards to each player, then places the next card face up on the table. Players, in turn, draw and discard one card, attempting to form compound words that they display in front of them. As in traditional rummy, they may choose to use the face-up card on the discard pile instead of drawing from the deck. Players wishing to use a card on the discard pile that is not on the top of the stack must also collect any cards discarded after the desired card. Play continues until one player uses all his or her cards to form compound words. If no player can accomplish this by the time the last card is drawn, the player with the most compound words wins that round.

#25

Drawing a Blank
(Newspaper)

BACKGROUND   When mature readers come to an unfamiliar term in their reading, they try to determine its meaning based on context. In a variation of this practice, if the unfamiliar word is removed, readers should be able to make sufficient sense of the sentence so they can substitute an appropriate word in the space to complete the thought.

ACTIVITY   Distribute copies of a news story, blotting out every seventh or eighth word. (Alternately, retype the story, replacing every seventh or eighth word with a blank line.) Avoid blotting out proper names or titles. Instruct students to read the passage completely, then reread it, filling in the blank spaces with words they think make sense. Hand out copies of the original article or display it on an overhead, and have students compare their substitutions with the original article. Discuss whether their words have changed the author's meaning.

Bibliography

Armbruster, B.B., C.H. Echols, and A.L. Brown. 1983. The role of metacognition in reading to learn: A developmental perspective. *Reading Education Report,* 40. Champaign: University of Illinois Center for the Study of Reading.

Baldwin, R.S., F.C. Ford, and J.E. Readance. 1981. Teaching word connotation: An alternative strategy. *Reading World,* 21:103–108.

Brophy, J.E. and C. Evertson. 1981. *Learning from teaching: A developmental perspective.* Boston: Allyn & Bacon.

Brown, A.L., J.D. Bransford, R.A. Ferrara, et al. 1984. Learning, remembering, and understanding. In *Carmichael's Manual of Child Psychology,* edited by P. H. Mussen. New York: Wiley.

Coman, M. and K. Heavers. 1990. *How to improve your study skills.* Lincolnwood, IL:VGM Horizons.

Doctorow, M.J., M.C. Wittrock, and C.B. Marks. 1978. Generative processes in reading comprehension. *Journal of Educational Psychology,* 70: 109–118.

Fogarty, R. 1997. *Problem-based learning and other curriculum models for the multiple intelligences classroom.* Arlington Heights, IL: IRI/SkyLight Publishing.

Gardner, H. 1993. *Multiple intelligences: The theory in practice.* NewYork: BasicBooks.

Linden, M. and M.C. Wittrock. 1981. The teaching of reading comprehension according to a model of generative learning. *Reading Research Quarterly,* 17:44–57.

Gipe, J. 1979. Investigating techniques for teaching word meaning. *Reading Research Quarterly,* 14:624–644.

Meichenbaum, D. and J. Asarnow. 1978. *Cognitive behavior modification and metacognition development: Implications for the classroom.* San Diego: Academic Press.

Ogle, D. M. 1986. KWL: A teaching model that develops active reading of expository text. *The Reading Teacher,* 39(6):564–570.

Pauk, W. 1974. *How to study in college.* Boston: Houghton Mifflin.

Richardson, J. and R. Morgan. 1994. *Reading to learn in the content areas.* Belmont, CA: Wadsworth, 1994.

Schumm, J. and M. Radencich. 1993. *School power: Strategies for succeeding in school.* Minneapolis, MN: Free Spirit Publishing.

Smith, F. 1976. Learning to read by reading. *Language Arts,* 53:297–322.

Stauffer, R.G. 1969. *Directed reading maturity as a cognitive process.* New York: Harper & Row.

Taylor, W.L. 1953. Cloze procedure: A new tool for measuring readability. *Journalism Quarterly* 30:415–433.

Wittrock, M.C. 1988. The cognitive movement in education. *Educational Psychologist,* 13:25–29.